Thai
Celebrations
FOR CHILDREN

text by Elaine Russell
illustrations by Patcharee Meesukhon

TUTTLE Publishing

Tokyo | Rutland, Vermont | Singapore

CONTENTS

Welcome to Thailand: Let's Have Some Sanuk! 4

Happy New Year! 6

National Children's Day 8

The Umbrella Festival 9

Chinese New Year 10

Chiang Mai Flower Festival 11

National Elephant Day 12

A Changing Symbol 13

To Protect and Preserve 13

Macha Bucha Day 14

Kite Competitions 15

A Temple Light Show 16

Boys Become Novices 17

The Fruit Festival 18

Chakri Day 19

Songkran Water Festival 20

Rice Growing Festivals 22

Buddha Day 24

The Ghost Festival   25

Let's Make a Ghost Mask   26

Dharma Day   28

The Candle Festival   29

The Drum Festival   30

The Diving Buddha Festival   31

Longboat Racing Festivals   32

Wrist-Tying Ceremonies   33

Buddhist Temple Fairs   33

The End of Buddhist Lent   34

The Lotus Flower Receiving Festival   36

Naga Fireball Festival   37

The Floating Lantern Festival   38

Let's Make a Loi Krathong Boat   39

Flying Lantern Festival   40

The Monkey Buffet Festival   42

A Northern Tradition   43

Thai Family Celebrations   44

A Thai Wedding   46

Welcome to Thailand: Let's Have Some Sanuk!

The people of Thailand love to have *sanuk*: that means fun! In the busy world of modern-day Thailand, holidays and festivals offer the chance to honor the nation's culture and history. Dancing, music and special foods are part of the fun. So let's fly a kite, join a parade or float handmade boats down a river. Whether it's Songkran New Year, a festival for monkeys or a family wedding, there's always a reason to celebrate.

Many Reasons to Celebrate

Most of the people in Thailand practice Buddhism. Many official holidays are important Buddhists rites. Other religious and ethnic groups—such as Muslims, Hindus and the people who live in the northern hills—have their own special holidays.

A Muslim Minority

Muslims make up about 5 percent of the population. They celebrate a range of holidays, including Islamic New Year, Eid al-Fitr (the end of the Ramadan fast) and Eid al-Adha, or the Festival of Sacrifice. While Muslims are found throughout Thailand, many live in the South.

Happy New Year! Wan Khuen Pi Mai

Fireworks light up the night sky with their colorful bursts. Bangkok (the capital and largest city) is a great place to celebrate the arrival of the new year on January 1. Hundreds of boats, barges and ferries glide down the Chao Phraya River. Floating on one is the perfect way to see the amazing show. Or go to the top of one of Bangkok's high-rises.

A Year's Worth of New Years

January 1 was made the official Thai New Year in 1940. But kids and their families also celebrate other related holidays: Chinese New Year, Thai Songkran New Year, the Islamic Awal Muharram celebration and those of other ethnic groups such as the Hmong, Akha, Lu, Lisu and Shan. With this many holidays, you can celebrate all year long!

Clothes for a Celebration

Boys wear a *chong kraben*, a large cloth wrapped around the waist and pulled up between the legs. It looks like loose-fitting pants. This is worn with a Nehru or raj-style shirt.

Girls usually wear a long tube skirt folded at the waist. Called a *pha sin*, it has a pattern along the bottom. On top, girls wear a simple shirt or a long scarf called a *sabal*. It's wrapped around the chest and over the left shoulder or worn over a blouse. Sometimes girls wear *chong kraben* as well.

National Children's Day

Wan Dek, or National Children's Day, is celebrated on the second Saturday in January. Events are held across the country: from petting zoos, magic shows and face painting to exhibits on robots and dinosaurs. Kids can make art projects or feed a giraffe a snack.

Just for Kids!

The focus is on kids having fun while also learning about things they might want to do when they grow up: fly a plane, become a doctor, work on a farm or help the environment.

ICE
cream

The Umbrella Festival

Artists in Bo Sang and nearby villages create beautiful umbrellas in a rainbow of colors. A bamboo frame is covered with saa paper (made from the bark of mulberry trees). The tops are then painted with designs. Flower, landscapes, elephants or dragons dance in the sun as the umbrellas are twirled round and round.

Made in the Shade

The people of Bo Sang hold an umbrella festival the third week of January. The day is filled with traditional music, drumming, dancing and lots of food. A parade includes women in traditional dress riding bicycles and holding umbrellas. Kids can also visit artists in their studios and see the umbrellas being made.

Chinese New Year

Out with the old, in with the new. The date for this celebration is set by the traditional lunar (or moon-based) calendar. So Chinese New Year usually falls between late January and the end of February.

An Explosion of Color

Parades fill the streets decorated with red lanterns. Banners offer wishes for good luck in the new year. People put on funny masks and carry delicate fans. Groups of men dress up as scary dragons or snarling lions. They dance, dip and slither along to the sound of Chinese drums and gongs.

Acrobats form towers, balancing on the shoulders of the person below them. Ribbon dancers swirl strips of silk through the air. To scare off evil spirits, firecrackers pop, as bursts of firework fill the night sky!

Chiang Mai Flower Festival

The warm climate in Chiang Mai Province is perfect for growing all kinds of flowers. Waves of color fill the fields. Orchids, hibiscus, jasmine and frangipani scent the air. Golden marigolds are often used as temple offerings. Lotus flowers, symbols of purity, are laid at Buddhist altars. Flower markets burst with blooms, and delicate garlands are sold in the streets.

Beautiful Blooms

The city of Chiang Mai is called the Rose of the North. It's known for a three-day flower festival, usually in early February. Flower displays of all sizes and colors line the streets. A parade of floats, made entirely of blooms, showing animals, temples and mythical figures also rolls by.

Thailand's National Flower

The bright yellow blooms of the golden shower tree were named the national flower in 2001. Called *don koon*, long clusters tumble off the branches like golden raindrops. The color yellow is important to Buddhists. It stands for harmony and unity.

11

National Elephant Day

These giant mammals and their handlers—called mahouts—are celebrated on March 13. Festivals are held in parks, zoos and camps. In some towns, monks bless the elephants and the people who gather to celebrate them.

Chang Thai Day

The elephants get to eat as much fruit, vegetables and sugarcane as they want. Kids can visit conservation centers where elephants are protected. There they live just as they would in the outside world. Visitors can help give the elephants a bath or feed them a treat.

A Changing Symbol

In the past, Thailand's elephants played many roles. They worked in fields and carried Thai armies into battle. As the modern world turned to machines, people relied on elephants less. They also faced a loss of habitat and the food it provides.

To Protect and Preserve

Thailand also celebrates World Elephant Day on August 12. It's a great time to visit a conservation center. They help protect the places elephants live in the wild. They also make sure the ones living in zoos get good care.

Makha Bucha Day

Macha Bucha usually falls in February or March on the full moon of the third lunar month. It marks the day when Buddha gave a special talk to a large group of monks hundreds of years ago.

Making Merit

Kids and their families head to their local Buddhist *wat*, or temple. They make merit, which means they perform good deeds. They bring food for the monks and leave flowers for Buddha on the altar. A *wian tian*, or candlelight walk, ends the special day. Everyone walks around the shrine carrying a lit candle, lotus flowers and incense to honor Buddha and the full moon.

Kite Competitions

From late February through March, the strong spring winds blow. So it's the perfect time to fly a kite! Festivals and competitions are held across Thailand, including the park in front of the royal palace in Bangkok. People from around the world bring their kites to join the fun.

Air Shows & Sky Wars

Three small towns in the South host popular international festivals. Kites shaped like cartoon characters, superheroes or animals soar through the sky. Stunt kites whip through the air at high speeds. Traditional Thai kites circle each other, trying to force the other team to the ground.

A Temple Light Show

In spring, a temple fair features a unique light show. It's held at Phanom Rung Historic Park in southeastern Thailand. Kids and their parents gather at dawn to walk the steep path up to the temple. As the sun rises behind it, light bursts through the 15 doors. A fiery glow fills the temple with more music and dancing.

Phanom Rung Temple Festival

In the park the celebration continues. Kids draw pink sandstone temples just like Phanom Rung. They watch as Thai dancers compete. Nighttime bring a sound and light show in front of the temple with music and dancing.

Boys Become Novices

The Tai Yai, or Shan, people in the North are known for a special three-day event in late March or early April. It celebrates when boys begin their training by becoming Buddhist novices (or students) of the temple monks.

Poi Song Long Festival

The boys are brought to the temple and dressed like young princes in outfits of brightly colored silk sewn with silver bells. The boys' heads are wrapped in silk decorated with flowers. Mothers put makeup on them.

After a blessing from the monks, the boys are carried on their fathers' backs to visit shrines. Special golden umbrellas shield them from the sun. On the third and final day, their heads are shaved. They then put on orange robes. For the next three months, they'll live and train in the temple.

The Fruit Festival

Have you ever eaten a longan? How about a rambutan or a mangosteen? Jackfruit, dragonfruit and rose apples are some of the other fruits found in Thailand. Guavas, papayas and coconuts grow year-round, while others only appear between early spring and late summer. That's the perfect time for tropical fruit festivals!

Sweet Celebrations

Chanthaburi Province is known as the "tropical fruit bowl of Thailand." In late May, it's home to a 10-day festival. Families visit orchards, sample fruit at buffets and view fruit sculptures. A highlight is the parade with floats made from fruit and flowers showing scenes from Thailand's history.

Durian—known as the "king of fruits"—is especially popular. Durian speed-eating contests are held. Fruit is on sale everywhere, in stalls and at the floating market.

Chakri Day

April 6 is the day to celebrate the Chakri royal family and the kings who have ruled Thailand. The royal family holds a ceremony at the Temple of the Emerald Buddha. Rama X, the current king, then honors the previous kings at the Royal Pantheon. He lays a wreath at the statue of Rama I at Memorial Bridge.

Honoring the Royals

To honor the day, people offer flowers to the king and his ancestors. Families visit their local temple to pray for them.

Other Holidays for the Royal Family

May 6—The coronation of Rama X, the king of Thailand
July 28—King Rama X's birthday
August 12—Queen Sirikit's birthday, also celebrated as Mother's Day
October 13—To remember the late King Rama IX, who ruled for over 70 years

Songkran Water Festival

Songkran is the biggest holiday of the year. Also called Water Days, it takes place from April 13 to 15. Kids pour scented water over the hands of their teachers and elders. They get blessings in return. Families visit temples where they wash the hands of monks. They also sprinkle water over Buddha statues to bring good luck.

Thai New Year

For many the best part of Songkran are the water fights! People throw buckets of water on each other or squirt super soakers. Even the elephants get in on the act. They fill their trunks with water and spray the crowds.

Rice Growing Festivals

Over half the people in Thailand are rice farmers. So the rice growing season is an important time of year. Festivals and ceremonies are held to honor farmers and bring good luck for plenty of rain and a good harvest.

Royal Plowing Ceremony

The Royal Plowing Ceremony takes place in mid-May. The Cultivating Ceremony is held on the first day. Monks bless the Lord of the Harvest, four Celestial Maidens, the royal rice seed, the paddy and a special ring and sword.

The next day the Plowing Ceremony takes place outside the royal palace. The Lord of the Harvest takes seeds from the Celestial Maidens' baskets and spreads them in the field. A team of white oxen helps finish the planting. The oxen are then given the choice of eating seven different foods. What they munch on predicts the crops that will be most successful.

Yasothon Rocket Festival

Giant rockets sail through the air, leaving a trail of smoke. Each May this Buddhist festival includes a contest. Which rocket can climb the highest? They are intended to get the attention of the rain god, *Phaya Thaen*, so there will be lots of rain to grow rice. The fun includes a parade and dancing to the music of gongs and *khaens* (bamboo flutes).

Buddha Day

Each May, Visakha Bucha Day honors Buddha. It starts with giving food to monks passing on the streets. Families set birds or fish free and listen to Buddha's teachings. At night, candles are placed around the temple. Like on Macha Bucha Day, a candlelight procession, or *wian tian*, ends the celebration.

The Ghost Festival

Bun Luang is the three-day celebration in the town of Dan Sai that features the Ghost Festival. The event mixes Buddhist tradition with local beliefs. It is meant to bring rain for the rice growing season.

Phi Ta Khon

Phi Ta Khon, or the Ghost Festival, kicks off the three-day event. Villagers of all ages wear colorful costumes and ghost masks made from rice husks and coconut leaves, topped with painted baskets decorated with bells. They march along and dance to music. The more noise the better.

Bursting rockets join the music and dancing on the second day. A prize is given for the best ghost costume. The scarier the better! On the final day, people sit and listen to the temple monks tell stories about Buddha and his teachings.

Let's Make a Ghost Mask

Phi Ta Khon ghost masks are made with the materials on hand. So add whatever you want to your own mask, make it as funny or scary as you like!

Materials needed:

Heavy white construction paper 18 x 24 inches (46 x 61 cm)

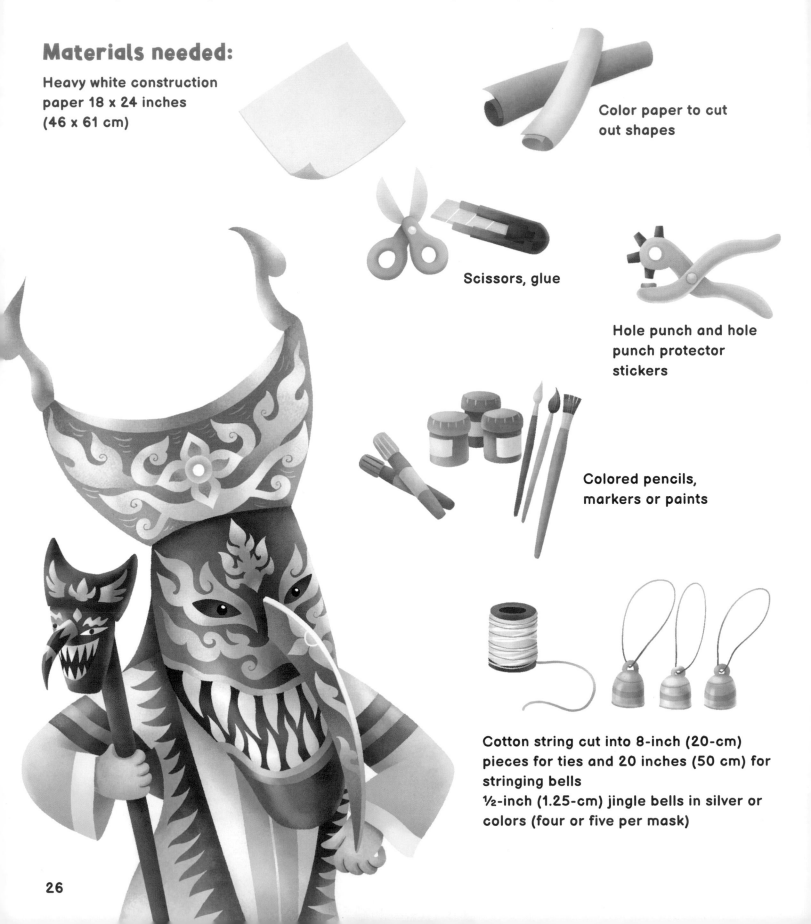

Color paper to cut out shapes

Scissors, glue

Hole punch and hole punch protector stickers

Colored pencils, markers or paints

Cotton string cut into 8-inch (20-cm) pieces for ties and 20 inches (50 cm) for stringing bells
½-inch (1.25-cm) jingle bells in silver or colors (four or five per mask)

26

Steps:

① Using the template, draw an outline of mask and separate nose.

② Cut out mask with openings for eyes and flap for nose. Then cut out separate nose.

④ Glue nose to nose flap on mask.

⑤ Punch holes at side of mask at eye level (for string ties) and just above forehead (to string the bells), and add hole punch protector stickers.

③ Color or paint the mask and nose, adding colored paper cut outs with glue, if desired.

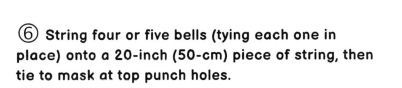

⑦ Tie 8-inch (20-cm) strings into punch holes at eye level and tie your mask on at the back of your head.

⑥ String four or five bells (tying each one in place) onto a 20-inch (50-cm) piece of string, then tie to mask at top punch holes.

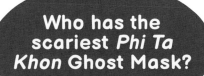

Who has the scariest *Phi Ta Khon* Ghost Mask?

Who can make the most noise?

Dharma Day
Asahna Bucha Day

At the end of July, families celebrate this holiday, honoring Buddha's first sermon to his followers over 2,000 years ago.

Honoring the Buddha

Khao Phansa is the day after Dharma Day. It's the start of the three-month Buddhist Lent, a time for monks to study and meditate. Many young men become novices then also. People travel to their ancestors' village to give offerings to the temple monks for their retreat.

The Candle Festival

The town of Ubon Ratchathani is known for its candles. A special festival celebrates them. Artists mold and sculpt huge floats out of wax for the Ashna Bucha Day parade. Temples and scenes from Buddha's life and Thai history move through the streets. Wax warriors, mythical figures, giant *nagas* (snakes), horses and elephants are part of the sights. The winner of the float contest is announced that evening.

The Drum Festival

Drummers march and play their instruments, as dancers move to the beat. A light and sound show in the evening tells the story of the "Legend of Drum Village."

Follow the Beat

In the village of Ekkarat, kids can watch craftsmen mold and shape rain tree wood into kettle and barrel drums.

The Diving Buddha Festival

The town of Phetchubun holds a festival at the start of the rice harvest. A local legend tells of farmers finding a Buddha statue floating in the river. They brought it to town where it disappeared twice. Each time it was found again in the river.

Bathing the Buddha

Called *Um Phras Dam Nam*, the festival celebrates the story of the Diving Buddha. At the start, the statue is carried through town. Offerings are made and sheets of gold are added to it. The statue is then brought to the river for bathing and blessings.

In the afternoon, longboat races are held. In one race, the teams have to row upstream.

Longboat Racing Festivals

Everyone loves the longboat racing festivals held during the rainy season from September to November. These races have been popular in Thailand for more than 400 years.

A Race to the Finish

Wooden longboats are narrow like kayaks, but much longer. The curved fronts are carved with decorations such as a dragon's head. The boats hold anywhere from 30 to 60 rowers. Teams row as hard as they can, gaining speed until one crosses the finish line first!

Wrist-Tying Ceremonies

On special occasions, family and friends tie cotton or silk strings around a person's wrist to wish them good fortune and protection. The ceremonies, called *baci*, are popular across Thailand.

Ties That Bind

Important events such as birthdays, weddings, graduations, New Year or the birth of a baby are almost always marked with *baci*.

Buddhist Temple Fairs

Temples play a key role in the lives of Thai Buddhists. Families go there to pray, make merit, learn Buddhist teachings and celebrate holidays. Most boys spend a few months as a novice at some point to earn merit for their families.

Family Fun

Local temples often hold a fair at least once a year. They include food, market stalls, games and entertainment. Larger temples even have carnival rides. Kids have the chance to sing and dance, performing for the adults.

The End of Buddhist Lent

Wan Ok Phonsa marks the final day of Buddhist Lent in October. Monks end their three months of study and meditation. It's a time for offerings as well as a time for festivals and races.

A Floating Light Show

Called *Lai Ruea Fai*, this event includes music, dancing and a contest for the best boat. The boats float along the Mekong River at night. Decorated with candles, lanterns, flowers and incense, they show mythical animals and scenes from Buddha's life.

The Chonburi Buffalo Races

In Chonburi, farmers honor the hard work of their water buffalos during the rice planting and harvesting season. A weeklong festival in October has parades, rides, games and food. But the buffalo races are the main event. The fastest beast wins. There are also contests for the decorated buffalo carts and the best-dressed buffalo.

The Lotus Flower Receiving Festival

Rap Bua takes place in Bang Phli at the end of Buddhist Lent. It's a tradition that started to welcome new people to the village. People gather along the canal to watch the beautiful barges float by. One carries a special Buddha statue. As the boat passes, people throw lotus flowers in the water, making a wish as they do. If the lotus lands near the Buddha, their wish will be granted!

Naga Fireball Festival

Each year near Nong Khai, people gather along the Mekong River to witness an amazing event. Thousands of fireballs burst from the water and soar into the night sky.

A Mysterious Sight

No one knows for sure the cause. Many Thai believe they're the breath of the *naga*, the mythical sea snake, which protects the river. Some scientists think it may be methane gas escaping and bursting into flame. Whatever the source, the fireballs are a wonder to see!

The Floating Lantern Festival

Thousands of flickering lights drift down the river under the full moon of a November night. After Songkran, this is many people's favorite holiday in Thailand.

The Lights of Loi Krathong

Loi Krathong has been celebrated for 700 years. Banana wood and leaf boats are sent off glowing into the night. It's a chance for a fresh start. The boats carry away the bad things from the previous year. They also bear good wishes and prayers for the year ahead.

The floating lanterns are a way of thanking Buddha and the Goddess of Water for a successful season. The boats are filled with flowers and incense. Some people add a coin or a lock of hair for good luck.

Let's Make a Loi Krathong Boat

Supplies

1 round paper maché box (7½ inch across and 3 inches deep—or 19 by 8 cm—available at craft stores)

7½ inch round of corkboard

Green construction paper

Pink construction paper

Fresh flowers in season (optional)

Glue

Double-sided tape

Ruler and pencil

Scissors

① Glue corkboard to the bottom of the paper maché box.

② Cut out green construction paper to cover sides and top of box and glue on.

③ Cut out paper petals and glue them to the side of box with the top 1/3 of the petals standing above the top of box.

④ Add fresh flowers or make a large lotus flower. (Cut out petals, bend at bottom, and glue to a small round base, alternating white and pink. Petals should stand up.)

⑤ Add a small candle in the middle, securing it with double-sided tape. If you like, use tape to add incense, a penny or nickel, and anything special you want to offer to the water goddess (like a special rock or shell).

Flying Lantern Festival Yi-Peng

Yi Peng, meaning "full moon day," takes place at the same time as Loi Krathong. As people float their candle boats down the river, they also send lanterns, or *khom loi*, into the night sky. In Chiang Mai and other parts of northern Thailand, the lanterns carry wishes to Buddha for good luck in the coming year.

Khom Loi

The lanterns are made from a bamboo frame covered in rice paper. A candle is placed in the center. The heat from the candle lifts the lantern into the sky. Hundreds of them glow in the night sky, as the lantern boats twinkle in the river below.

The Monkey Buffet Festival

In late November, the town of Lopburi treats its furry, long-tailed residents to a feast. More than 3,000 monkeys gather on the grounds of Pra Sam Yot Temple. Huge tables with red tablecloths are loaded with platters of fruit, vegetables, sticky rice, raw crab and Thai desserts.

A Well-Fed Bunch

Locals believe the monkey buffet brings good luck. The monkeys are often fed in the town, and they're never shy. They'll come up and grab food right out of people's hands!

A Northern Tradition

In the far north of Thailand, the village of Doi Hua Mae Kham is home to many different ethnic groups. Known as the hill tribes, the Akha, Lahu, Lisu, Tao, Hmong and Tai Yai have their own languages, crafts, food and traditional clothes and customs.

The Hill Tribe Sunflower Festival

As the weather turns cooler in November, sunflowers burst into bloom in the hills. The hill tribes celebrate with music, dancing, craft sales and special local foods.

Thai Family Celebrations

Thai families have special ceremonies for important events and moments in life. Getting married, welcoming a new baby or having a birthday all present the perfect reasons to celebrate.

It's Your Birthday

Kids in Thailand don't always have birthday celebrations. Thai people typically visit a temple to make offerings. Thai life is split into 12-year cycles. Later birthdays, such as 60 or 72, are more likely to be celebrated by family and friends. However in recent years, kids' birthday celebrations have become more common. Presents and cake are a part of the day, along with treats to share at school.

A New Baby

Children are usually given their name on the fourth or fifth day after birth. When they're one month and one day old, a *khwan*, or hair-shaving ceremony, is held. A monk shaves the baby's hair except for a small patch on top. The hair is then placed on a banana leaf raft. A lotus leaf and flowers are added. The family then sends the raft downstream, offering good wishes for the baby's life. *Khwan*, or cotton strings, are tied to the baby's wrists and ankles for protection.

A Thai Wedding

An engagement ceremony is held at the future bride's home. Monks bless the couple who serve the monks food and make offerings to Buddha and the bride's ancestors.

The wedding ceremony often takes place at a hotel. The groom's family and guests arrive in a procession. They bring flowers and food for the bride's family.

The Shell Ceremony

The bride and groom then sit or kneel before small tables. A family elder places two cotton hats, or *mong koi*, tied by a string, on the couples' heads to join them for life. After that comes *rod nam sang*, or the shell ceremony. Family and friends pour water from a shell over their hands. Then it's time to party! Guests enjoy a feast, games, music, dancing and sometimes karaoke. They also offer advice for a happy marriage.

Author's Dedication

I want to thank Warunee Prommanuwat, Thai studies teacher at the NIST International School in Bangkok, for her suggestions on celebrations to include in this book. She is always so kind to give me her attention and time. As always I am grateful to my husband and family for their support. And a big thank you to Patcharee Meesukhon for her wonderful illustrations and to editor Douglas Sanders and all the team at Tuttle Publishing.

Published by Tuttle Publishing, an imprint of Periplus Editions (HK) Ltd.

www.tuttlepublishing.com

Text © 2022 Elaine Russell
Illustrations © 2022 Patcharee Meesukhon

Library of Congress Cataloging-in-Publication Data in process
ISBN 978-0-8048-5280-7

25 24 23 22   10 9 8 7 6 5 4 3 2 1

Printed in China   2111EP

Distributed by

North America, Latin America & Europe
Tuttle Publishing
364 Innovation Drive
North Clarendon, VT 05759-9436 U.S.A.
Tel: 1 (802) 773-8930; Fax: 1 (802) 773-6993
info@tuttlepublishing.com
www.tuttlepublishing.com

Asia Pacific
Berkeley Books Pte. Ltd.
3 Kallang Sector, #04-01
Singapore 349278
Tel: (65) 67412178; Fax: (65) 67412179
inquiries@periplus.com.sg
www.tuttlepublishing.com

"Books to Span the East and West"

Tuttle Publishing was founded in 1832 in the small New England town of Rutland, Vermont [USA]. Our core values remain as strong today as they were then—to publish best-in-class books which bring people together one page at a time. In 1948, we established a publishing office in Japan—and Tuttle is now a leader in publishing English-language books about the arts, languages and cultures of Asia. The world has become a much smaller place today and Asia's economic and cultural influence has grown. Yet the need for meaningful dialogue and information about this diverse region has never been greater. Over the past seven decades, Tuttle has published thousands of books on subjects ranging from martial arts and paper crafts to language learning and literature—and our talented authors, illustrators, designers and photographers have won many prestigious awards. We welcome you to explore the wealth of information available on Asia at **www.tuttlepublishing.com**.